The Glass is 100 Per Cent Full – Lifting Out of Anxiety and Depression

by Susan Haslam

Best wishes and God bless

Love Susan
xx

CONTENTS

INTRODUCTION

'Brighter Days' by Emili Sandé

On February 14th, 2017, I was hospitalised for being in a hypomanic state and was diagnosed with bipolar disorder. The psychiatrist said that I was too happy and needed to take medication to bring me down to a normal state. I had engaged in a lot of things which on their own would not have been out of the ordinary behaviour, but together, they indicated to my friends and family that I was behaving strangely. One of the things I had done was buy 15 Valentines' Day cards; I wrote one each for my daughter and son, one for myself, one for my future partner as I was single at the time, and the rest I gave to the other patients in the psychiatric unit. I went up to each person, asked what their name was and wrote a card out to them. Their reactions were a mixture of surprise and appreciation, and looking back, I think this was a lovely gesture and I am really glad I did it.

I was in and out of hospital for a couple of months until I had come down and started operating at a 'normal' level, and agreed to take the medication I was prescribed. I was very much against taking medication at first and wanted to come down naturally, but this was against what the psychiatrists require for bipolar disorder which is classed as a chronic condition. My sister also told me about her research into the condition and explained that a hypomanic episode is the equivalent of a heart attack of the brain. That certainly brought home the seriousness of what I was going through.

I had left my job and returned home really pleased with the idea of having some time updating my home and seeing more of my children. However, what followed was a period of anxiety and depression that I had never experienced before. I was then very keen to take anti-depressants but I was told by the mental health worker that this wasn't possible as there was a risk I would go too high again.

It took nearly a year to lift out of the depressed and anxious state I was in and I was able to start another job in January 2018. This helped to build my confidence and the following March I was feeling much better and decided to stop taking my medication for managing my bipolar disorder. I told my psychiatrist and he said that I seemed to be doing okay but bipolar was a chronic condition and the medication was needed for life. I struggled to accept this and wanted to be living medication-free. However, four months later I had another hypomanic episode and was again hospitalised. This was similar to the first experience of being on a high and living without normal boundaries. I would liken it to being very happily drunk.

This was again followed by a period of anxiety and depression which lasted many months. I eventually got back to a normal state until the Covid pandemic hit and I fell into a depressed and anxious state worse than I had ever experienced. I tried anti-anxiety medication but it didn't work for me. This time, I didn't even have the hypomanic episode, I went straight to a low.

My second hypomanic episode was caused by me stopping taking my medication as I had a desire to be medication free but which I later accepted as key to my balanced mental health. However, this only stops the highs. I then started reading and researching all the things I could find that would help to lift me out of anxiety and depression to address the lows.

One of the main reasons I wrote this book was to have in one place all of the ways I could find that have lifted my spirits and to share it with other people having a similar experience. I have a Masters Degree in Spiritual Psychology and I have also included some of my key learnings from my studies in this book, which, I admit, I had lost touch with during my middle age but I have started applying again in my life now.

We can't control the thoughts that enter our minds but we can choose what we focus on. The content of this book aims to help us focus on uplifting things in life. Our feelings follow our thoughts, so thinking better helps us to feel better. There are several ways that help to give us peace of mind, to reduce stress and increase our levels of happiness. This involves stimulating all of our senses in a positive way.

The main thing I have learned is that it is important to have a whole arsenal of uplifting practices in our lives. Consequently, when a problem or stressful event occurs, which inevitably it will, we will have a strong safety net in place to cushion the fall. Having a collection of destressing and uplifting practices supports us in shifting from fearful thinking to living at the heart of our being where love is the dominant force.

I have also learnt that having balance is key. When I was hypomanic, I was doing some of the ways set out in this book to an extreme and when depressed and anxious, I wasn't doing nearly any of them at all. I have experienced spiralling upwards and spiralling downwards. Whilst doing the uplifting things to the extreme during the hypomanic episodes was not a good thing, when done in moderation, they can help lift out of a depressed state. Consequently, practicing many of these things in moderation has helped me the most with having a balanced, positive and strong attitude to life.

When I was low, the things that bring us peace, love and joy inside ourselves and noticing them in the outside world too just weren't on my radar. This book is a collection of 40 different ways to rediscover these positive emotions which I hope will inspire you, motivate you and lift you up and out of anxiety and depression. I am not medically recommending them but I have learnt that as I added these things to my life, the anxiety and depression lessened until one day I woke up and they were gone. There was a tipping point at which there was more positivity in my life to overcome the fear-based thoughts and replaced them with the power of love for my life.

Read the following pages with a pen to hand and tick those boxes where you already include them in your life or tick the boxes where you think you would benefit from adding them to your life. Adding positive actions to your life, even just micro steps, is key; as well as making the decision to lift out of anxiety and depression.

Chapter 1

LISTENING TO UPLIFTING MUSIC AND SINGING AND DANCING

'Shut Up and Dance' by Walk The Moon

At the start of my first hypomanic episode, I had taken my children to watch the movie "Trolls" which had some great songs in it. When we returned home we played and danced to these songs some more. This was something I did because of being in a hypomanic episode – I was listening and dancing to a lot of tunes. My room was a Disco. The brilliant thing about phones these days is that they give us access to songs on YouTube or Spotify. Alternatively, Smart speakers such as Alexa make listening to music so easy. A gentler version of having uplifting music in our lives is enough to raise our spirits.

There was a young lady in the room next to mine when I was in hospital and she had lots of marks on her arms and neck from self-harming. She played a song for me which was a sad song and I asked her to show me her playlist and the only song I recognised as an uplifting and energising song was Meatloaf's "Paradise by the Dashboard Light" so I asked her to play that and we both danced and had some fun. Looking back, we helped to balance one another out in those moments together. I was brought down to reality and she was laughing and experiencing some happiness.

When we feel sad, we may want to listen to a song that reflects our mood but it doesn't help when we feel really low. Having a playlist of empowering and uplifting songs can really help with how we feel and operate in life. For example, boxers and darts players enter the room to their own favourite and empowering tune to perform better in their matches. Do you have a song or songs that make you feel good?

In this book rather than put in quotes which many personal development books have, I have listed a song at the beginning of each chapter which I find uplifting and I encourage you to create your own power list of songs. I play these when I am in the shower, doing the cleaning and before I start work.

Singing along to our favourite songs and dancing to them adds to the uplifting experience which we can do in the comfort of our own home.

Do I already practice this in my life?   □

Would I benefit from adding this to my life? □

Chapter 2

ACTS OF KINDNESS

'Treat People With Kindness' by Harry Styles

There's a link between kindness and wellbeing. It is known that acting kindly makes us feel good and people who carry out more kind acts have higher levels of wellbeing, on average.

Something I occasionally do is buy the person behind me in the queue in a coffee shop their drink. I once got talking to a couple in a café where I was having breakfast and the guy paid for my breakfast saying that was his good deed for the day completed. It was great being the subject to someone else's act of kindness. Introducing acts of kindness to those around us as well as ourselves brings positive benefits into our lives even small things like holding the door open for the person behind you.

Being kind isn't just about actions, it is also about the things we say and think. Looking for the good in ourselves and in others helps to shift away from negative thinking. We can't control the thoughts that come into our mind but we can choose what we focus on. Choosing to be kinder in our thoughts will be followed by being kind in what we say and what we do. Committing to one act or thought of kindness a day is a positive step in contributing to lifting ourselves up.

Do I already practice this in my life?

Would I benefit from adding this to my life?

Chapter 3

MEDITATION

'Heaven Is A Place On Earth' by Belinda Carlisle

When I experienced anxiety and depression during the Covid lockdown, I was at my lowest. I hadn't had the hypomanic high beforehand I just went low. I was staying in my bedroom, except for meal times, and I just had to lie down on my bed in foetal position feeling really scared. It was during this time that I started researching ways to lift myself out of the dark place I was in.

From the material I read, meditation often came up as a way to lift out of anxiety and depression and this was something I had dabbled with in the past but never developed it into a practice. I started meditating with my mum just for five minutes a day for a week at first and I did this lying on my bed as sitting up on a chair was too big of a challenge for me. My mum sat on a chair next to me and we listened to some meditation music. The following week we increased it to 10 minutes and kept increasing by five minutes each week until we reached 25 minutes.

Both my mum and I felt the benefits of this and although my anxiety and depression didn't go away completely, they were noticeably reduced and I was no longer spending most of my time in my bedroom.

We carried on the practice downstairs in the living room for 15 minutes each morning as we felt the benefits of meditating for even this shorter length of time.

My meditation practice involves focusing on my breathing and saying, "I am at peace," in my mind. Meditation is a key way of learning to focus the mind in a positive way and detach from negative and fearful thought patterns. This is a major practice to add to your arsenal of ways to lift out of anxiety and depression.

Do I already practice this in my life? ☐

Would I benefit from adding this to my life? ☐

Chapter 4

PRAYER

'Higher Love' by Kygo and Whitney Houston

I first started praying in the hospital chapel when I came down from my first hypomanic episode. Before then, I hadn't prayed since primary school during assemblies. For the first time in my life, I felt I needed to start praying for help and I found it very soothing and calming. It helped to lift some of the weight off my shoulders and let go of the guilt I felt about the mistakes I had made in my life. I was praying to God and the Universe.

The church I attend have a prayer team who prayed for me whilst I was in hospital. When I am going through a challenging time in my life, I ask my Christian friends to pray for me. Likewise, I pray for them when they need support. I pray in the mornings but some days have a 'pray as I go' practice.

The Bible says the following:

> "Do not be anxious about anything, but in every situation, by prayer and petition, with thanksgiving, present your requests to God. And the peace of God, which transcends all understanding, will guard your hearts and your minds in Christ Jesus." **Philippians** *Chapter 4*, Verses 6 to 7

Praying to God, a higher power or the Universe is incredibly powerful and is also one of the twelve steps of Alcoholics Anonymous.

There isn't a right or wrong way to pray but as the above Bible section advises – say what you are thankful for and what you need or want in your life or pray for other people you know are struggling and need support. It is also about listening to any response that comes to mind. It feeds our higher self to help bring solutions to problems or to give us peace and strength as we go through them.

Praying is amazing and even more so because it is free. Both prayer and meditation have been found to have the same positive effects on the brain so doing both is really going to help lift us up.

Do I already practice this in my life? ☐

Would I benefit from adding this to my life? ☐

Chapter 5

EXERCISING

'Jump' by Van Halen

Exercising is key to lifting us up and releasing feel-good hormones in our bodies. I am a member of a gym which has a swimming pool and I love swimming to relax and raise my spirit. When I went low after my two hypomanic episodes, I made myself exercise most days and this helped me to get through each day.

When the Government introduced a lockdown during the Covid pandemic and gyms were closed, this had a hugely detrimental impact on people's mental health, including mine. This led to me doing a lot more research into things that help to reduce depression and anxiety. When I was at my lowest, finding the motivation and energy to do any exercise was really hard. I started by walking just 100m along the road from my house and I did this each day. I felt like I was carrying a huge weight around with me. I then added 10 minutes of yoga in my bedroom and increased that every week. It was small incremental steps that I built up over time. I was incredibly relieved when the health clubs were able to open again.

I now exercise every day which is a mixture of walking my dog, yoga, swimming or working out in the gym. My friend Michael, who is a partner in a law firm, works out every morning before starting work and says he trains for his mind, not his body as it helps him with difficult cases. There are many different sports we can engage in either as a team or individually. Adding this into your life pays dividends for your mental as well as physical health. Just walking 30 minutes a day will have a positive impact on your wellbeing.

When my daughter was struggling with her mental health, she was only doing physical education once a week at school and she didn't really enjoy it and wasn't doing any out of school activities. She said she would do cycling classes at the gym but she was a few months below the minimum age to do the gym classes. She was old enough to go to the gym, but she said she didn't want to do that. I really felt that her having an exercise regime in her life would help her. I suggested a number of different sports and eventually she said she would try the gym. She really enjoyed it and we got into the routine of her going three times a week. This lifted her up immediately and we have made it a regular part of her feel-good routine.

Do I already practice this in my life? ☐

Would I benefit from adding this to my life? ☐

Chapter 6

MULTI-GENERATIONAL LIVING

'We Are Family' by Sister Sledge

When I came out of hospital the first time, my family realised how much I was struggling to cope with my life and with managing my children. Having discussed things with my parents we agreed that they would move in with my children and me. My son was 5 at the time and my daughter was 8 and I can still remember the weight that was lifted off my shoulders when this happened. It was just the help I needed in looking after the children and running a home.

Once I was better, we decided that we would all continue living together as we worked well as a team. We shared the chores and the bills which was really helpful as a single parent. It is great to be living together during the good times having survived living through the bad times.

I used to be lonely every night when my children had gone to bed, but since my parents moved in with me the loneliness went away. Feeling lonely contributed to the stress I was under that led to my bipolar disorder.

British culture is generally about children becoming independent and moving out of the family home but in Italy and Spain and some Asian countries, multi-generational living is commonplace. Children, parents and grandparents living together and pooling resources and abilities can increase our quality of life.

Do I already practice this in my life? ☐

Would I benefit from adding this to my life? ☐

Chapter 7

LIFE COACH

'Barcelona' by Freddie Mercury and
Montserrat Caballé

I have used a life coach a number of times including before I was diagnosed with bipolar disorder at times when I was feeling stuck. I found this really helpful. Having another person to help me gain clarity and direction was worth the money. They aren't cheap but if you can afford it, it is definitely worth adding as a string to your bow of personal growth and upliftment.

One of the life coaches I used in the past was a spiritual lady and I found the sessions very healing. Another life coach I used was more focussed on action steps to take to address the issues. Taking small positive action steps can have dramatic impacts on our lives and this is why I would highly recommend starting with one or two measures set out in this book that aren't already in your life; this alone will improve your mental and emotional wellbeing. Then, as your energy and motivation levels increase you can add more. This eventually tips the scales in favour of a more positive state of being.

I have also chosen a life coach who prays for me

as I am a strong believer in the power of prayer. The last life coach I used also pointed me to the following quote from the Bible which really helped me:

> "For God has not given us a spirit of fear, but of power and of love and of a sound mind."
> **2 Timothy** *Chapter 1*, Verse 7

Do I already practice this in my life? ☐

Would I benefit from adding this to my life? ☐

Chapter 8

WATCHING FUNNY MOVIES

'Happy' by Pharrell Williams

One of the things I did when I was going through a hypomanic episode was watch funny and uplifting movies and there were several that I watched multiple times. These were, It's a *Wonderful Life*, *Sister Act* and *Groundhog Day*. This was part of the extreme nature of the episodes and as with all of the practices, doing them in moderation is key. Laughing is very therapeutic and we laugh more when we are with other people who are laughing. When feeling low, watching a comedy with someone else is a definite way to lift yourself and feel good. Here is a list of movies that have had me in stitches:

- *It's a Mad, Mad, Mad, Mad, World;*
- *The Great Outdoors;*
- *Dirty Rotten Scoundrels;*
- *Dinner For Schmucks;*
- *National Lampoon's Christmas Vacation;*

- *Date Night;*
- *Planes, Trains and Automobiles;*
- *Hot Fuzz;*
- *Johnny English;*
- *Airplane;*
- *There's Something About Mary;*
- *Shallow Hal;*
- *Naked Gun;*
- *Bridesmaids;*
- *Hangover;*
- *Blades Of Glory;*
- *Best In Show* and
- *Blazing Saddles.*

Do I already practice this in my life?

Would I benefit from adding this to my life?

Chapter 9

FOOD AND HERB- AL SUPPLEMENTS

'Good Feeling' by Flo Rida

During my research, I found five supplements to take to help attain good mental health. The two I continue to take daily are magnesium and cod liver oil for Omega-3 fatty acids. The other three which have been found to be of benefit are St. John's Wort, lavender and ashwagandha. Always consult your doctor on whether to take any supplement, especially if suffering from any conditions or taking any medication.

Magnesium helps reduce anxiety and may help with depression. It also helps with our energy levels which tend to be low during anxious and depressed periods. Magnesium also has been shown to reduce the stress hormone, cortisol.

Omega-3 fatty acids have many benefits including helping with mood disorders and anxiety.

St. John's Wort is nature's answer to anxiety and low mood. This herb is known to help mild to moderate depression due to the chemicals in it that helps the serotonin receptors in the brain, and serotonin is key to promoting feelings of wellbeing and happiness. It has also been found to help sleep better and improve memory. In Germany, it is used as a first line of treatment for depression. Expect the benefits to be felt after about four weeks.

There are very few side effects to St. John's Wort but it can reduce the effectiveness of blood pressure medication and contraceptives, so it is recommended that you consult your GP before taking this herb. It also isn't recommended for people with bipolar as it can trigger a hypomanic episode so I chose not to take it.

Lavender is a common herb which can be taken in a tablet form to treat anxiety and mental stress. Having a cup of lavender tea before bedtime provides a much safer and natural alternative to medications. I didn't try this as my medication has a sedative effect and I fall asleep very quickly.

One herb I did try was ashwagandha which is used in traditional Indian medicine. It has been used for thousands of years to relieve stress and increase energy levels. I took it for a few weeks when I was getting better but decided not to continue taking it as I was satisfied with the progress I was making from my other practices.

Do I already practice this in my life? ☐

Would I benefit from adding this to my life? ☐

Chapter 10

GROUP SEMINAR EVENTS

'I Love Rock 'N' Roll' by Joan Jett & the
Blackhearts or Britney Spears

I have attended a number of personal growth seminars, both before and after my bipolar diagnosis, and have found these to be really powerful and energising. There is something about the dynamic created when a group of people come together – it can work miracles. It supports connecting to our higher, intuitive selves and accessing our personal power.

I would recommend attending support groups such as mental health groups or personal development courses. These include in-person or online events that can be attended from the comfort of your own home. I think in-person sessions are better but online ones are still very effective.

Participating in these events is like going on holiday to the best part of yourself. I found the various seminars and courses I participated in to be empowering, informative and healing as well as helping me with breakthroughs in my life.

Do I already practice this in my life? ☐

Would I benefit from adding this to my life? ☐

Chapter 11

SUNSHINE

'Walking On Sunshine' by Katrina and the Waves

In my research on bipolar disorder, I read that many people have a hypomanic episode in the Spring which coincides with days getting longer and there being more sunshine. Of the two hypomanic episodes I experienced, one was towards the end of Winter and the other at the start of Summer. A hypomanic episode is experiencing intense happy emotions and this is why I believe sunshine and spending time outside can help lift someone out of feeling low and depressed.

A holiday in the sun is a great pick me up, especially in the winter months. This is important as so many of us work indoors on computers these days.

Exposure to sunlight helps our bodies to naturally produce Vitamin D and it is known that this Vitamin might play an important role in regulating mood and reducing the risk of depression. Going for a walk for 30 minutes a day has the double benefit of exercise and getting enough Vitamin D. I take Vitamin D supplements during the winter months when we have less sunlight and I believe this helps to support my mental and emotional health in line with what studies have shown.

We can also use a sunlamp in the winter months which friends of mine who suffer from Seasonal Affective Disorder say really helps them. This is another way of our skin producing Vitamin D.

Do I already practice this in my life?

Would I benefit from adding this to my life?

Chapter 12

LEARNING SOMETHING NEW

'What A Wonderful World' by Louis Armstrong

When I went through my first hypomanic episode, I went to the supermarket and bought about 40 magazines on every subject there was. I had a real thirst for knowledge on many different subjects including gardening, dogs, health and wellbeing, and economics. I came away with two large bags of magazines, one of which my sister took back to the store for a refund as she was concerned about my spending spree.

Learning something new in a subject we are interested in stimulates us and engages our mind in a positive way. Magazines just cost a few pounds and have the most up to date information on a subject, and often have interviews with experts in that field.

Going to the library gives us access to free books and there is also information on the internet that is freely available.

I like to buy a magazine or a book and go to a coffee shop by myself and just sit and read. It is a really relaxing pastime and I am stimulating my mind in the process.

Just think of a subject or hobby you are interested in or were interested in in the past and buy a book or magazine on that subject. If nothing comes to mind, then go into a bookshop or look at the magazines rack in your supermarket for inspiration. The breadth of knowledge available is remarkable.

Do I already practice this in my life? ☐

Would I benefit from adding this to my life? ☐

Chapter 13

GOING TO THE THEATRE AND CONCERTS

'You Raise Me Up' by Josh Groban or Westlife

As part of my spending spree during my hypomanic episodes, I bought a lot of theatre tickets. I hadn't been to the theatre or to a concert in about five years and I purchased tickets for the musicals: *Sister Act*, *Bat Out Of Hell* and *Grease* which were showing over the following year. This is an example of my extreme behaviour and there is no need to fill out your diary with concerts or shows to feel the uplifting effect of this. Just one or two shows a year is all that is needed.

I appreciate tickets for major productions aren't cheap but as an occasional treat going to live events is an uplifting experience to raise the quality of our lives. Watching shows by local amateur dramatics groups or cover bands are cheaper and still provide an uplifting night out.

Festivals are also a great experience to immerse yourself in fabulous music over a few days. There is also the anticipation and excitement leading up to a concert to see your favourite artist perform.

I also like going to see comedians, which are an

alternative to a play or musical performance. The Edinburgh festival is a fabulous event filled with comedy and enough to lift anyone's spirits.

Do I already practice this in my life? ☐

Would I benefit from adding this to my life? ☐

Chapter 14

WEARING PERFUME OR COLOGNE

'Diamonds' by Rihanna

During my second hypomanic episode, I bought three bottles of perfume. A further example of taking things to the extreme. Smelling good suddenly became more important as I had stopped wearing perfume years before. I gave one bottle to my daughter who had never had perfume before and kept two for myself.

When I smell good, I feel good and this makes sense as our sense of smell is directly linked to our limbic system and our brains react to any scent we put on our body.

I recall going to a shop post-Covid with a screen on the counter providing just a small hole for exchanging goods and money and the lady commented on how nice my perfume was. Smelling good is similar to looking good which boosts our self-confidence.

Perfume and cologne are a popular stocking filler at Christmas between lovers and for those of you who are single treat yourself to a nice scent to lift your mood.

Some perfume oils have been shown to relieve stress. These include:

- Lavender oil;

- Bergamot oil; and

- Lemon oil.

Spraying your pillow with perfumes including lavender or bergamot oil can also help you to relax and fall asleep.

Do I already practice this in my life?   ☐

Would I benefit from adding this to my life? ☐

Chapter 15

SHOPPING

'Stronger' by Kelly Clarkson

During both of my hypomanic episodes I went on a spending binge. Buying things you love or need feels good. However, I did this to an extreme and I would recommend this is done moderately to combat anxiety and depression. I took my children to a large toy store, gave them each a basket and said they could have whatever they wanted. They were over the moon. My daughter found an electronic dog that was expensive and asked if that was okay and I just said no problem. I had recently acquired a credit card and it was all fine. When their baskets were full, I paid for them and we went home and spent the whole day playing with their toys. It was one of the best days we had ever had together.

One of the other extreme things I did was go to a Tesla car showroom and I ordered a Model X with every single optional extra included. It was incredibly expensive and I paid the small deposit using my credit card which was all that was needed. I was confident that the money would come to me to pay the remainder but it never did. I was hospitalised soon after and my sister contacted Tesla to cancel the order and ask for the deposit to be returned. My psychiatrist also wrote a letter to explain my situation. Tesla discussed it at their next board meeting and agreed to return the deposit. This has increased my respect for them and to own a Tesla is still on my list of life goals.

I now have a small budget each month for shopping for treats as it feels good. For small budgets, bargains can be had on some internet sites and at car boot sales and in charity shops. Items to buy include clothing, something for the home or even perfume or cologne as mentioned in the previous chapter.

I would strongly recommend not buying things on credit as it is not good for our financial wellbeing which I talk about later. My credit rating was badly affected by my excessive spending and not being able to repay my debts. Buying things that are in your budget is key to getting the benefit of this practice.

Do I already practice this in my life? ☐

Would I benefit from adding this to my life? ☐

Chapter 16

GUT HEALTH

'Three Little Birds' by Bob Marley and the Wailers

When one of my friends found out about my ill health, she recommended that I look at my gut health. I did some research and this definitely stood out as an area I could improve. I had a poor diet for many years which included a lot of sugary snacks.

The gut is home to trillions of bacteria (known as the microbiome), both good and bad, and if you have ever had antibiotics, this can have a negative impact on your gut health. I was particularly interested in this as I read that our gut bacteria help to regulate mood and manufacture about 95 per cent of the body's supply of serotonin, which is key to regulating our mood.

My friend recommended a 21-day gut health program which I knew would benefit me but this seemed like too big a challenge for me and so I put it off. I did, however, take some probiotic supplements to help put some good bacteria into my microbiome.

A few years later, after I had my third experience of depression and anxiety, I looked again at my gut health and started having live natural yoghurt every day. This and kefir are recommended to add good bacteria to our gut and I noticed that my skin started to look much better. I have rosacea which often flares up when I am stressed but it significantly reduced after about a week. I also started to feel more positive.

I was still sleeping 10 to 12 hours a night and decided to look at a gut health program to really address any issues in my microbiome that were affecting my energy levels. I was also clear that I didn't want to be depressed and anxious again and felt I had the motivation to do the gut health program a friend suggested.

The 21-day program I followed included protein shakes, multi-vitamins and minerals, and probiotics. I had to cut out dairy, alcohol, caffeinated drinks, wheat, rice, pasta, starchy vegetables and sugary snacks. I had one meal a day consisting of protein, vegetables and salad. Yogurt and fruit were allowed. After about seven days, I was feeling much healthier. I went down to eight hours of sleep a night and was waking up before my alarm wanting to get up and face the day. I started feeling much more motivated about my life. My energy levels increased significantly.

When I reintroduced the foods back into my diet, I noticed that I did sleep longer but my motivation for life has stayed with me. I still have no problem waking up in the morning and getting out of bed ready to face the day. This was a major learning point for me and I will definitely be doing a gut health program once a year going forward.

I would recommend either improving your diet to aid better gut health or undertaking a gut health program for increased benefits.

Do I already practice this in my life? □

Would I benefit from adding this to my life? □

Chapter 17

FORGIVENESS

'Don't Look Back In Anger' by Oasis

Forgiveness was one of the key tools I learned during my Masters in Spiritual Psychology. Some people think that forgiving someone for the thing(s) they did or said lets them off the hook or that it makes it ok, but it isn't about the other person. Forgiveness is the most selfish thing we can do as it is letting go of the judgement we are carrying inside about ourselves, others or even God. It is the judgement itself that has a negative impact on our wellbeing.

I was really angry with the mental health service for putting me in hospital as it separated me from my children, but looking back, I was doing a lot of extreme stuff. I also didn't want medication, I wanted to come down naturally so I was really angry that I was forced to take the medication by injection. I later came to forgive them and saw that this was the best way to treat my condition. I also needed to get on with my life and free myself from the past and forgiveness helps to do that.

During my third depressed period, I was aware I was feeling ashamed of myself about the bad choices I had made in my life. I chose to forgive myself for judging myself as a poor decision maker and a poor mother and decided to learn from my mistakes. We know ourselves better than anyone else and taking responsibility for our life now and using forgiveness to let go of the things in our lives that hold us back is one of the best tools we have to lift ourselves up.

Do I already practice this in my life? ☐

Would I benefit from adding this to my life? ☐

Chapter 18

SELF-CARE

'Rise Up' by Andra Day

Self-care is really important. If you look good, you feel good. Looking after ourselves and our appearance was encouraged during my Masters Degree in Spiritual Psychology, which also taught me that outer experience is a reflection of inner reality. Improving our relationship with ourself is really important.

During my hypomanic episodes I was really motivated to improve my appearance. I was showering twice a day, I was booking appointments with my local health and beauty salon for facials, pedicures, manicures and having my hair cut and styled. I had my colours done to find out which colours of clothing would suit me best and which styles. I even started the process for having braces to straighten my teeth.

When I fell into a depressed state on the other hand, my self-care dropped too. I was showering twice a week and my motivation and energy to look after myself had really lapsed. I did read that we don't need to shower every day to save on water unless we have been exercising or doing manual labour which made it okay in my mind to let go of my shower routine. However, when I have showered, I felt fresh and energised.

My hypomanic episodes followed by depression meant that my selfcare routine went from one extreme to the other, but over the years I have learnt to treat myself to beauty treatments now and again and to have regular trips to the hair salon as these things make me happier with the way I look. I finally got braces for my teeth, five years after my first hypomanic episode, as I was actively looking to complete some of the goals I had outstanding from that time.

Personal care products for men are much more common these days supporting men to also take more care over their appearance to feel good too. I noticed the number of men with unkempt beards increased rapidly during the Covid lockdown. These can look very smart when groomed and treated with oil or cream to make them soft. This makes kissing a man on the cheek much nicer too!

I strongly recommend taking time to help yourself to look good and consequently, feel good about yourself.

Do I already practice this in my life? ☐

Would I benefit from adding this to my life? ☐

Chapter 19

PETS

'You've Got The Love' by Florence and The Machine

One of the items on my 'to do list' when I was having my first hypomanic episode was to get a dog. I had a dog when I was a child but my children had never had a pet. I guess I didn't want the responsibility and I worked in an office so I didn't want a pet being left home alone all day.

My daughter really wanted a dog, though, and when I had been working from home for a few years and could see that continuing, I decided it was a good time to get one. It was four and a half years after my first hypomanic episode that we finally got a Pomeranian. She has really added to the love and joy in our home. My parents were very much against getting a pet and my dad came up with every reason under the sun not to get one, but even they have fallen in love with her.

Taking her for a daily walk has helped with my fitness levels and taking her out rain or shine has benefited me even more.

It is known that pets support good mental health. Having a dog has definitely helped to lift my mood. Just looking at her cute little face makes me feel good. Dogs are always so happy about going for a walk or having their food, and are always really pleased to see us when we come home. A pet is a constant companion and helps with loneliness.

If you can afford to keep a pet and take on the responsibility, then having a pet is another way to help with mental wellbeing.

Do I already practice this in my life? ☐

Would I benefit from adding this to my life? ☐

Chapter 20

SWEARING

'abcdefu' by Gayle

One thing that I started doing during my first hypomanic episode was swearing in front of my closest friends which surprised them. I didn't swear at all prior to this, but I found it released negative energy inside of me and added more emphasis to what I was saying. Studies have shown that cursing helps to relieve physical pain and emotional stress.

When my daughter started secondary school, she said that all of the kids swear and she swore too at school. Secondary school kids are often mean to one another so I can understand them wanting to swear so much.

One of my church leaders, who doesn't swear, was telling the story about how he broke his foot at work and it was the one time he swore. His colleagues were more interested in the fact he had sworn than his broken foot.

If you don't already swear, then when you are feeling stressed or angry about someone or something include some swear words when talking about it and feel the benefit of it lightening the load. Anxi-

ety and depression are fucking awful and thank fuck
I have gotten over them.

Do I already practice this in my life? ☐

Would I benefit from adding this to my life? ☐

Chapter 21

WORK

'9 To 5' by Dolly Parton

Surveys have shown that most people are unhappy in their job and I was one of them. I was working five days a week with a long commute which was very stressful and a significant contributor to the onset of my bipolar disorder. A few months before my first hypomanic episode, I agreed with my employer to do a four-day week. This helped to relieve some of the stress I was under but it was too little too late.

When I experienced my first hypomanic episode, I handed my notice in feeling positive that every-thing would work out ok, but I had no new job to go to and my family were worried about my financial sit-uation. I was tired of my profession and said I didn't want to go back to that line of work.

However, when I recovered from the anxious and depressed state that followed the hypomanic state, I started looking for a job in my profession as it paid well and I was the sole provider for my family. I did some gratitude exercises and focused on what I did like about my job. I managed to get a job working from home and four days a week which was ideal for me. Although it wasn't my heart's calling, it paid the bills and was better than me wasting my time doing nothing.

Having a job helped to occupy my time, keeping me busy and taking my mind off my fear-based thoughts. I had a lot of anxiety when I was starting a new project, but I found that by getting on with my work rather than succumbing to the fear, the work got easier and my confidence grew. The anxiety started to subside and fade into the background rather than dominating my thoughts. Consequently, I became stronger in myself.

During the Covid lockdown, I was furloughed and not having a job to do gave my mind too much time to think and I fell into an anxious and depressed state for the third time. On the plus side, it was during this time that I reflected on my life and looked at the different ways to lift myself up. I also started doing a small number of hours of voluntary work at a local food bank to help with that charity and give myself something to do. This also helped me to feel better.

I have found that adding more positive things to the rest of my life helps me to have a better attitude towards my work. Doing a four-day week also helps with my work–life balance. Whether paid or voluntary, it helps us to contribute to society and in turn that helps to build our self-worth.

Do I already practice this in my life? ☐

Would I benefit from adding this to my life? ☐

Chapter 22

GRATITUDE

'Giant' by Calvin Harris and Rag'n'Bone Man

I have used gratitude journaling on and off for a number of years and have always found this helpful at lifting me up. I find it most helpful to do at the start of my day to perk me up.

My job was something that I felt I wanted to change as my heart wasn't in it and so I focused on the things I was grateful for about my job. I wrote them down on a piece of paper and placed it on my desk where I could see it; it helped me to have a happier disposition towards my work.

I also started a gratitude exercise with my daughter. Whilst walking home from school, we would share three things we were grateful for. One could be a repeat from a previous day and two of them had to be new.

Studies have shown that a gratitude practice helps to lift our mood as it focuses our mind on the good things in our lives. Starting a gratitude journal to write down your list of things you are grateful for or picking someone in your life to share them with are both great ways to put this into practice. I felt the benefits of this straight away as it shifted my mind to positive thinking.

My sister was a huge support for me during my ill health. She told me that every family has someone with a major health issue and thanked me for taking the hit for our family!

Do I already practice this in my life?   ☐

Would I benefit from adding this to my life? ☐

Chapter 23

SETTING GOALS AND HAVING A PURPOSE

'Firework' by Katy Perry

Having a purpose in life and setting goals gives us a reason to live and get through depression and anxiety. During my hypomanic episodes I had loads of energy and was writing long to do lists and seeking to achieve a lot. This contrasted hugely with my anxious and depressed state when if I had anything to do, it felt overwhelming and difficult.

To combat my depression, especially when I was in my lowest place, I had two purposes I was striving for. The first was to be the best mum I could be to my two children and the second was to be the person helping others rather than being the one needing help.

I was also told by a friend that anxiety is a warning from the unconscious mind to focus on what you want so focus on what you want. Writing down what you want to achieve in your life helps to give you a positive focus and direction. For this exercise, I would recommend writing a list of 10 goals and putting it somewhere you look at regularly such as in your wallet/purse or on your bedside cabinet. Ticking them off as they are completed gives us a sense of achievement and satisfaction.

I created a vision board which I placed on my bedroom windowsill so I saw it each day when I opened and closed the curtains. I bought a vision board from my local arts and crafts shop and they are also available online. I then found words and pictures from the magazines I had bought to provide a collage of all the things I wanted in my life.

Do I already practice this in my life? ☐

Would I benefit from adding this to my life? ☐

Chapter 24

MAKING LOVE

'Locked Out Of Heaven' by Bruno Mars

Making love to a partner or ourselves is a pleasure of life that helps to relieve stress and makes us feel good. I had been single for four years when I had my first hypomanic episode and hadn't made love in all that time. At the start of my first hypomanic episode, I booked a trip to London with the aim of meeting someone to have sex with but I was hospitalised beforehand unfortunately/thankfully!

I recall working in a large open office many years ago and my colleague came in walking on cloud nine and announcing that he had morning sex. He was so happy he couldn't contain himself. There was no response from the rest of us but I remember thinking 'good for him'.

We may not feel like making love but going ahead with it anyway can then put us in the mood for it. Include this once a week into your positive lifestyle practices and you will reap the benefits to your body and mind.

Do I already practice this in my life? ☐

Would I benefit from adding this to my life? ☐

Chapter 25

TRUST IN GOD / THE UNIVERSE

'Running Up That Hill' by Kate Bush

I have learnt to trust in God that everything will turn out ok as it always does in the end and if it isn't ok, it isn't the end. The two times I was in hospital I couldn't understand why I was there as I just felt great. Looking back, I did need support as my mind was in overdrive and I was imagining things that weren't reality. The anxiety and depression I experienced after each hypomanic episode and during the Covid pandemic were incredibly challenging.

During my third low period a church friend pointed me to the following verse in the Bible which I feel was key to my getting better and staying well by trusting in God:

> "You will keep in perfect peace those whose minds are steadfast, because they trust in you."
> **Isaiah 26:3**

I wrote 'Trust in God' in large letters on a piece of paper and put it on my bedroom wall as a daily reminder.

I later came across the following verse which is even more inspiring:

> "But blessed is the one who trusts in the Lord, whose confidence is in him. They will be like a tree planted by the water that sends out its roots by the stream. It does not fear when heat comes; its leaves are always green. It has no worries in a year of drought and never fails to bear fruit." **Jeremiah** 17:7-8

This was a revelation to me, because I realised that especially with anxiety, I was experiencing the opposite of peace. By trusting God with my life, it gave me faith that I could handle my problems. It is by overcoming problems that we become stronger and more able to handle life's difficult periods.

The other verse from the Bible that gave me faith was:

> " 'For I know the plans I have for you,' declares the Lord, 'plans to prosper you and not to harm you, plans to give you hope and a future.' "
> **Jeremiah** *Chapter 29*, Verse 11

I have learnt from one of the personal development courses I did to know that God/the Universe is working to support us and is not against us and to trust in the process of life.

Do I already practice this in my life? ☐

Would I benefit from adding this to my life? ☐

Chapter 26

HOBBIES / PASTIMES

'Spice Up Ur Life' by the Spice Girls

How we spend our recreational time can have an impact on how we are feeling. The world is full of a wide variety of wonderful things to occupy our time. In this digital age, there is so much available online as well as in the physical world.

My favourite pastimes are reading and home improvements and I also like playing word games and puzzle solving games which are apps on my phone. I find these relaxing and they add joy to my life. They also engage my mind in a positive way rather than being occupied with fearful thoughts. I also like watching TED talks that are available online which are inspirational and motivational.

Hobbies can involve being with others if you are looking to increase your social network and like being with other people. Alternatively, if you are looking to charge your batteries by being alone then there are a lot of things to choose from as well.

Here are some that I am aware of that might inspire you to take up one if this is an area in your life you want to improve on: buying and selling items online, bowling, arts and crafts, chess, backgammon, solitaire, bridge, DIY, reading, writing, collecting or

fixing cars, supporting a sports team, learning a musical instrument, photography, supporting a charity,
joining a book club, public speaking, trainspotting,
jigsaw puzzles, collecting stamps, coins, etc., bird
watching, planting trees, fishing and knitting.

Do I already practice this in my life?

Would I benefit from adding this to my life?

Chapter 27

THERAPY

'Hold My Hand' by Jess Glynne

There are a number of different therapies available to help with anxiety and depression. I chose Cognitive Behavioural Therapy (CBT) as this was recommended by my consultant and has been shown to help these conditions. Other therapies include Neuro Linguistic Programming, Hypnotherapy, Psychotherapy and Art Therapy. I would recommend speaking to your doctor about what is available to you and which you feel would best help you.

I had eight sessions of CBT over the phone which worked for me as leaving home felt like too big a challenge at the time. I didn't experience any major breakthrough from this but I did feel some benefit and the main thing I learnt was to challenge my negative thinking.

Having time with someone who is focused and experienced in helping you to get better is a tried and tested solution. It supports us and gives us tools for healing the past and dealing with life going forward.

Do I already practice this in my life? ☐

Would I benefit from adding this to my life? ☐

Chapter 28

DRINKING TEA

'I Gotta Feeling' by The Black Eyed Peas

The benefits of drinking water are well known but I do like a warm drink during the cold months so I looked into the benefits of different teas for good mental health. During my gut health program, caffeinated drinks weren't allowed and excess caffeine can cause anxiety so choosing teas that don't contain caffeine is recommended. However, a combination of caffeine and L-theanine found in both green and black tea has been shown to help our mood. Green tea has lower amounts of caffeine than black tea and also has many other benefits.

Other teas that benefit our mental health that do not contain caffeine are as follows:

1. Chamomile tea – helps with relaxation and sleeping;

2. Lavender tea – supports feeling calm and sleeping;

3. Ashwagandha tea – supports feeling calm;

4. Lemon balm tea – supports improved mood and sleeping;

5. St. John's wort tea – helps with anxiety and depression;

6. Peppermint tea – helps to deal with stress and anxiety

I drank peppermint tea, green tea and chamomile tea when I was at my lowest and found them very soothing. I now drink a glass of water first thing in the morning followed by a cup of English breakfast tea and that helps me to start my day well and get my mind focussed on what I need to do. I drink peppermint tea from mid-afternoon onwards.

Do I already practice this in my life? ☐

Would I benefit from adding this to my life? ☐

Chapter 29

PATIENCE AND ACCEPTANCE

'This Is Me' from The Greatest Showman

I felt like I was in a battle with the anxiety and depression I was experiencing and I just wanted to get rid of them. And quickly. In one of my sessions with my life coach, he suggested that, instead, I embrace them. This was a revelation to me and it really changed my perspective on how to deal with what I was thinking and how I was feeling. In my Masters Degree in Spiritual Psychology, I learnt to have conversations with parts of my mind to see what they are trying to tell me and to learn from them. I decided to try this with my anxiety and depression.

I had a number of areas in my life I was upset about including being a single mum and the line of work I was in wasn't my heart's calling. Addressing these parts of my life taught me t lessons of patience and acceptance. I was also reminded of the following serenity prayer:

> "God, grant me the serenity to accept the things
> I cannot change, courage to change the things

I can, and wisdom to know the difference."
Reinhold Niebuhr (1892-1971)

I learnt to focus on the aspects that I did like about my work and accepting as an important part of my life. I tried dating websites as that was me taking action but I came to accept being single and being ok with that.

The biggest lesson for me was being patient for the anxiety and depression to lift whilst taking positive action steps.

Do I already practice this in my life? ☐

Would I benefit from adding this to my life? ☐

Chapter 30

A ROMANTIC PARTNER

'Burning Love' by Elvis Presley

One of the major factors to my high level of stress was being a single, working mum. It was about four years after my relationship had ended that I was diagnosed with bipolar disorder. On reflection, if my relationship had worked out, I don't think I would have had the stress that led to my bipolar disorder.

Being in a good relationship and having a husband or wife who are committed to staying together whatever the weather has a positive impact on our wellbeing. I have found that being single is better than being in a bad relationship but being in a loving, supportive relationship is better than being single. Working as a team with a compatible partner helps us to achieve so much more in life. It says the following in the Bible:

> "Two are better off than one, because they have a good return for their labour. If either of them falls down, one can help the other up... Though one may be overpowered, two can defend themselves. A cord of three strands is not quickly broken." **Ecclesiastes** *Chapter 4*, Verses 9, 10 and 12

Finding a marriage partner is one of the blessings of life but there is still plenty of joy to be had in life whilst being single.

Do I already practice this in my life? ☐

Would I benefit from adding this to my life? ☐

Chapter 31

COLD SHOWERS

'Unstoppable' by Sia

Cold water plunges or showers have been found to improve our mental health. Training your mind to withstand the cold for up to three minutes helps to build resilience. I have found that switching my water temperature to cold for even ten seconds at the end of my shower, wakes up my senses and empowers me for the day. I do this just a couple of times a week. Increasing our tolerance to cold water in this way helps to strengthen our mind to deal with stressful events in our lives. Endorphins are also released when having cold showers leading to us feeling happier and positive.

Do I already practice this in my life? ☐

Would I benefit from adding this to my life? ☐

Chapter 32

FINANCIAL STABILITY

'Money, Money, Money' by Abba

I was experiencing significant financial stress prior to my bipolar disorder. I had a loan, a credit card, car loan, high mortgage payments with more money going out than coming in each month. My children were in private education so I had high payments for that as well. These payments were comfortable when I was with my ex as we were both on good incomes but trying to continue them on my own was stretching my inner elastic band too far. This was definitely key to what caused my mental breakdown with stress being a major cause for bipolar disorder.

When I came out of hospital the first time, I had no job and my care coordinator recommended I contact a debt charity. This led to me going on a Debt Management Plan and I was just paying one pound a month to each of my debtors. I made the decision to take my children out of private school and felt a huge weight lift off my shoulders.

Six months later I found another job working from home and just four days a week which was perfect for me to get a happy work/life balance and increase my debt repayments. Fortunately, the bank that gave me the loan decided to write off the debt.

A year later, the debt charity I was using helped to agree a lower amount of money than I owed to finalise the Debt Management Plan. My parents lent me the money for this. I did have a poor credit rating as a result and it would affect my ability to get credit for another five years but it was a good lesson in better managing my finances.

I had also bought a cheap car for not much more than I was paying in a year on my car payments. It is still running well four and a half years later. I reduced my outgoings so that I had ten per cent of income free each month to start saving and have been doing this for a couple of years now.

If your finances are great then brilliant but if you need help then contacting a debt charity for free help is a positive step forward to helping with your mental health. There are several debt charities available which offer support in this area. Years later, having spoken to a debt counsellor about improving my credit rating which was badly affected, she found a credit card that I was able to get to build up my credit score. I just use it to buy fuel for my car and pay it off each month.

Do I already practice this in my life? ☐

Would I benefit from adding this to my life? ☐

Chapter 33

AFFIRMATIONS

'Titanium' by David Guetta ft. Sia

I have definitely found benefit from saying affirmations either out loud or silently in my mind. I say them in the shower, whilst exercising or when I am out walking. Quite simply, they are significantly better than fearful mind chatter. I found saying one for five to ten minutes a day beneficial.

Some examples of affirmations are below. You can use them as they are or adapt to your own preference:

"Every day in every way, I am getting better and better," by Emile Coué;

"Be still and know that I am God," **Psalm** 46:10;

I am trusting myself that I will handle my life;

I am strong;

I am powerful;

I am loving and accepting myself;

I am bringing forth peace, love and joy to myself; and

I am safe.

Use or adapt one of the above with the qualities you would like to have in your life. When life is hard, that is when we learn to dig deep within ourselves to find inner resources and to become stronger and more powerful. We all have access to God and the Universe to help us to handle life's challenges.

Do I already practice this in my life? ☐

Would I benefit from adding this to my life? ☐

Chapter 34

HOLIDAYS

'Holiday' by Madonna

During the Covid lockdown when I was experiencing my third bout of anxiety and depression, I decided I wanted to take my children on a road trip to the south-west of England. We planned the trip for the start of their summer holiday when things would be opening up again. We had only had a couple of short holidays over the previous few years due to limited funds and I just felt we needed time away and to have some fun.

We visited Wookey Hole and Glastonbury in Somerset, the Eden project in Cornwall and went to Alton Towers Theme Park on our way back. During our holiday, the anxiety and depression lifted. My mind was focussed on driving and the new places we were seeing. It took my mind off my life back home and most importantly it got me out of my bedroom where I had been spending a lot of my time. It was just six nights away and it did us all a world of good. When we got back home, I did have some anxiety and depression return but it wasn't as bad as before.

This experience taught me the importance of having time away to recharge my batteries and see beautiful parts of the world. It is known that there are benefits to having holidays as they lower our stress levels and improve sleep quality, blood pressure and emotional wellbeing. Just having a holiday to look forward to supports feeling good so booking a holiday in advance rather than last minute is a positive step in lifting your spirits.

Do I already practice this in my life? ☐

Would I benefit from adding this to my life? ☐

Chapter 35

SUPPORT NETWORK

'Don't Stop Me Now' by Queen

Having a good support network was key to me getting better and staying well. This can be friends, family, support groups and spiritual or religious support. I am fortunate to have support from all of these and having them to get through difficult times helps me to lighten my load and succeed in life. It was also really nice to hear them say how well I was doing when I got better and stronger.

Living with my parents meant they saw me the most when I was really low and this was hard for my mum as it would be for any parent when their child is struggling whatever age they are. However, just having them be strong for me lead the way for me to become strong too. I liked hearing about times when they had struggled and got through it such as when my dad was made redundant and they only had my mum's small wage coming in.

Sharing difficult times with friends is healing. "A problem shared is a problem halved," is a wise saying. When my anxiety was at its worst, I struggled to sit still especially in the mornings and my right knee wouldn't stop tapping up and down so I would have to keep moving to release the nervous energy in my body. I would go to church and during the service I would be pacing at the back of the hall as I just couldn't sit down. I would share what I was going through with my church friends and they would pray for me and by doing this they helped me to get better.

Building connections with people can take time, but meeting up regularly with family and friends will help the bond grow and will have a positive impact on your life and theirs too. When you get stronger and start thriving then this puts you in a great place of understanding and empathy to help other people.

Do I already practice this in my life? ☐

Would I benefit from adding this to my life? ☐

Chapter 36

BREATHING

'Life' by Haddaway

The way we breathe has the power to relieve anxiety and stress, and focussing on our breath helps to take our attention away from negative mental chatter. Slowing down our breathing and taking deeper breaths has a soothing effect.

There are a number of different breathing techniques but the one I found the best is used by American Navy Seals known as box breathing. Navy Seals have to deal with high stress situations, so this is a great way to help with anxiety. I use this breathing technique when I am having treatment at the dentist.

A guide for box breathing as I practice it is as follows:

Step 1 – Inhale slowly through your nose while mentally counting to four. Focus on filling your lungs and abdomen with air. Notice how your body feels as you do this.

Step 2 – Hold your breath and mentally count to four again.

Step 3 – Exhale slowly through your mouth while mentally counting to four. Focus on getting all of the air out of your lungs.

Step 4 – Hold your breath and mentally count to four again.

Repeat the process until you feel calmer and more relaxed.

Do I already practice this in my life? ☐

Would I benefit from adding this to my life? ☐

Chapter 37

HOME ENVIRONMENT

'A Spoonful Of Sugar' from Mary Poppins (1964)

Having a clean and tidy home environment is something I have always maintained. In Feng Shui, your home represents your mind so keeping your home in a good state is important. I am a minimalist when it comes to my home but it was starting to look tired when I had my first hypomanic episode. During this time, I updated mine and my children's bedrooms and added more colour to these rooms.

When I was in a hospital, I had a meeting to review whether I was ready to be discharged and the independent psychiatrist asked about the state of my room, and the answer was 'clean and tidy'. When I was struggling with depression and anxiety, I still stuck to my house cleaning routine, although finding the energy to do it was hard at that time. Maintaining a good home environment is ingrained in me no matter how ill I may feel. Being surrounded by an uncluttered space and with items that I love and enjoy looking at supports me in feeling good.

Instilling this discipline in my children is important. Before I give my children their pocket money, they have to tidy and vacuum their bedroom. My son had lots of items such as pieces of Lego and clothing scattered on the floor. He would also hide his things under the furniture so that it looked tidy at first glance and so an inspection of his room also requires looking under his bed. My daughter keeps her room tidy throughout the week to make it easy to tidy at the weekend, however, I noticed my son was quite happy living in a messy space throughout the week. Therefore, I changed the rules for him that a portion of the pocket money depended on daily tidying. I am sure his future partner will thank me for this discipline!

Do I already practice this in my life? ☐

Would I benefit from adding this to my life? ☐

Chapter 38

COLOURS

'Somewhere Over The Rainbow' by
Israel Kamakawiwo'ole

The colours we see around us have the power to affect our mood and energy levels. During my first hypomanic episode I brought a lot more colour into my home and in the clothes I was wearing.

Spending time in nature and seeing more green helps to reduce our stress levels. I spent more time in my garden and I bought some plants and flowers for my living room. It is known that we are more creative when surrounded by green plants and scenes of nature.

After working from home for a few years, I realised I could place the desk and chair in front of the window looking out on to the grass and trees which provided a much better view when taking a break from my screen. Having a picture of a green landscape can also be beneficial.

I painted my kitchen walls blue which is my favourite colour. This is a colour which reminds me of the sea or a clear sky and helps me to feel calm.

Feelings about colours are subjective and also related to the culture we live in. Some colours have positive connotations in some countries whilst having sad connotations in others. Therefore, incorporating the colours you personally like to look at into your environment has the power to lift your spirits and promote calmness.

Do I already practice this in my life? ☐

Would I benefit from adding this to my life? ☐

Chapter 39

HAVING FAITH

'Amazing Grace' by Celtic Woman

Both of my hypomanic episodes had a strong spiritual side to them and I felt close to God. I spoke to the hospital chaplain and I started to think about faith. I remembered reading that people who have a strong faith and religious community live longer than those without faith which I thought was a strong testament for having a religion.

I had always classed myself as a spiritual but not religious person, but once I was well again, I decided I wanted to get my children Christened. We found a local church that was very traditional but didn't feel like the right fit for us. We then found another church which was a Pentecostal church and they had a live band singing gospel songs either side of the sermon. My children and I liked it so we made it our regular Sunday morning event to go there. It appealed more to us than the first church we tried which sang traditional hymns.

The church community was really supportive especially when I was hospitalised again during my second hypomanic episode.

Christianity is the right faith for me but I respect the following of all faiths. Billions of people adhere to the major religions of Christianity, Islam, Hinduism, Buddhism and Judaism. What I have learnt from going to church and from the friends I have made there is that it doesn't make you immune from having problems but it does provide you with a belief that things are going to be alright. There is an inner contentment that comes from having faith.

One of my favourite quotes from the Bible is:

"But the fruit of the Spirit is love, joy, peace, forbearance, kindness, goodness, faithfulness, gentleness and self-control. Against such things there is no law." **Galatians** *Chapter* 5, Verses 22 to 23

Having faith also provides connection to a likeminded community of supportive people which enriches our lives. I strongly recommend exploring different faiths to see if you feel a calling towards one.

Do I already practice this in my life? ☐

Would I benefit from adding this to my life? ☐

Chapter 40

CHOCOLATE

'The Candy Man' by Sammy Davis Jr.

Whatever state I have been in, I have always considered chocolate cake to be one of the best things in life. It is well known that chocolate helps us to feel good. Consuming cocoa releases the four feel-good neurotransmitters of dopamine, serotonin, endorphins and oxytocin. Dark chocolate has more cocoa than milk chocolate but can taste bitter. There is also caffeine in cocoa so milk chocolate contains less and white chocolate doesn't have any caffeine in it. Given the link between caffeine and anxiety, this is something to enjoy in moderation. I abstained from chocolate and sugary treats during my gut health program, but wow did chocolate taste great when I had it again.

Do I already practice this in my life? □

Would I benefit from adding this to my life? □

NEXT STEPS

'Get The Party Started' by Pink

I learnt from my life coaching sessions and Insight Seminar that the Universe rewards action. Just doing one positive thing can have a dramatic ripple effect in your life. I started off by meditating for five minutes and over time added more positive actions and I got more energised, motivated and less anxious and depressed. The cumulative effect of taking these actions helped me to get well again and reach a point where I could handle stressful events in my life. Doing these positive steps tips the scales in favour of loving thoughts rather than fearful thoughts.

Look back at those chapters where you ticked that you consider you would benefit from adding these actions to your life and pick one to get started. Congratulate yourself on the positives you already have. God helps those who help themselves and you are the best person to help yourself and so it is really important to take action in your life to support your mental and emotional health.

You may also have inspiration to do other things not listed in this book that will bring more joy into your life. I would especially recommend that you do those things that you feel anxious about. Doing the things that we are fearful of expands our mind and helps us to become stronger, and builds our self-confidence.

Write down below your list of what you can add to your life that you are willing to commit to doing and set a date for when you are going to do them.

Printed in Great Britain
by Amazon